Sound It

PATRICIA ALLPORT

Drawings by Jana Rodger

1

Oliver & Boyd

Designed by Thomas Campbell

Oliver & Boyd
Robert Stevenson House
1/3 Baxter's Place
Leith Walk
Edinburgh EH1 3BB

A Division of Longman Group Limited

ISBN 0 05 003810 9

First published 1985
Third impression 1988

© Oliver & Boyd 1985

Printed in Malaysia
by Percetakan Jiwabaru Sdn. Bhd., Bangi, Selangor Darul Ehsan.

Contents

sh

sh	sh	sh	sh
sheep	shop	shelf	ship

Write

1. The —— is in the water.
2. —— give us wool.
3. Put the book on the ——.
4. The —— sells lots of things.

Draw a shell.

sh

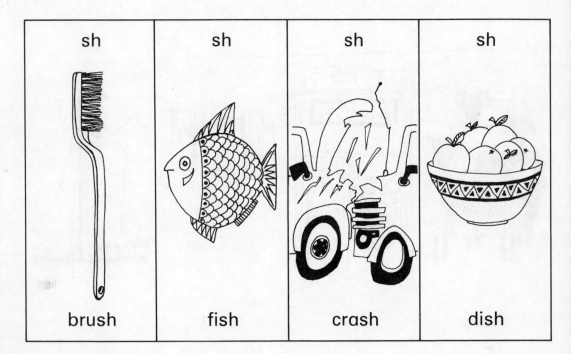

sh	sh	sh	sh
brush	fish	crash	dish

Write

1. The —— swims in the sea.

2. Six apples are in the ——.

3. The two cars had a ——.

4. We use a tooth —— to
   clean our teeth.

Draw a bush.

ch

ch	ch	ch	ch
chair	child	cheese	church

Write

1. I am a ———.
2. We go to ——— on Sunday.
3. I sit on a ———.
4. The mouse likes the ———.

Draw a big chimney.
Write a sentence about it.

ch

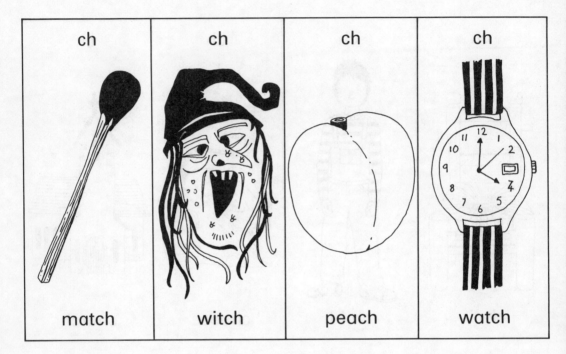

ch	ch	ch	ch
match	witch	peach	watch

Write

1. The ——— has an ugly face.
2. I like to eat a ———.
3. My ——— tells me the time.
4. We use a ——— to light the fire.

Write a sentence using these words

1. patch   2. catch

Find the word

a   b   c   d   e   f   g   h

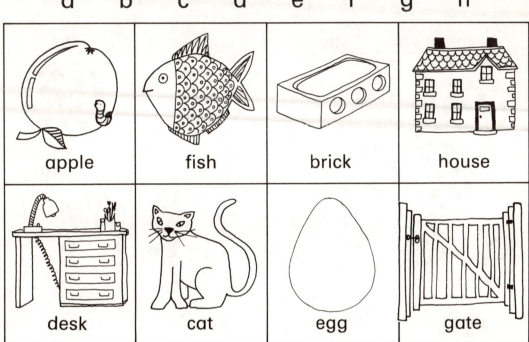

apple   fish   brick   house

desk   cat   egg   gate

Write

a   is for ———.   e   is for ———.

b   is for ———.   f   is for ———.

c   is for ———.   g   is for ———.

d   is for ———.   h   is for ———.

a   b   c —— —— f   g ——

a —— —— d   e —— —— h

th

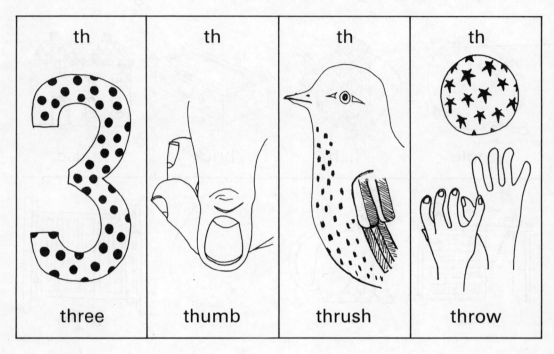

th	th	th	th
three	thumb	thrush	throw

Write

1. A ——— is a little bird.
2. I have a ——— on my hand.
3. My lucky number is ———.
4. I can ——— a ball.

Draw three thin things.

wh

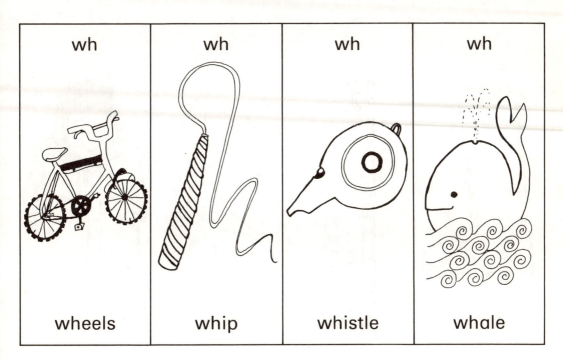

wh	wh	wh	wh
wheels	whip	whistle	whale

Write

1. The policeman blows his ———.
2. A ——— is a very big fish.
3. There are two ——— on my bike.
4. The ring master cracks the ———.

Write a sentence using the word wheat.

oo

oo	oo	oo	oo
boot	hook	moon	book

Write

1. I put my coat on a ——.
2. The —— comes out at night.
3. I like to read my ——.
4. My —— is on my foot.

Draw a foot and write a sentence about it.

oo

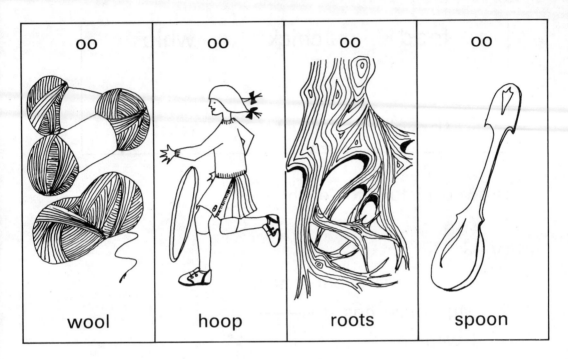

oo	oo	oo	oo
wool	hoop	roots	spoon

Write

1. The tree has lots of ———.
2. I use a ——— to eat my food.
3. My jumper is made of ———.
4. The girl plays with her ———.

Write sentences using

1. pool   2. cook

Read these words

food   chick   whip

three   shirt   roof

Draw a picture for each one.

Write
1. A ——— is a baby hen.
2. My house has a ———.
3. I wear a ———.

Now you have to write a sentence for

4. whip
5. three
6. food

Find the word

i j k l m n o p

lorry	ink	nest	kettle
pie	orange	jug	mop

Write

i is for ———.   m is for ———.

j is for ———.   n is for ———.

k is for ———.   o is for ———.

l is for ———.   p is for ———.

i j —— —— m n —— p

i —— —— l —— —— o ——

15

Animal noises

squeak squeak

miaow

hee haw

quack quack

bow wow

tweet tweet

baa aa

cluck cluck

Write

1. The donkey says ———.
2. The dog says ———.
3. The cat says ———.
4. The duck says ———.
5. The hen says ———.
6. The bird says ———.
7. The mouse says ———.
8. The sheep says ———.

ee

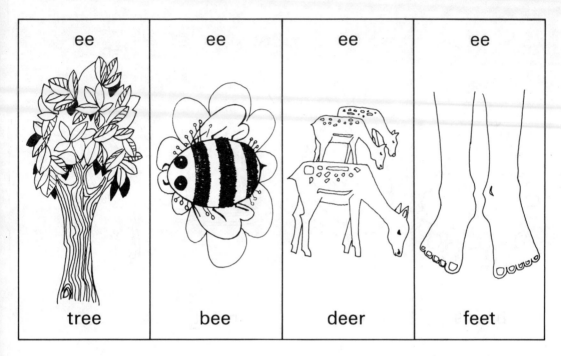

ee	ee	ee	ee
tree	bee	deer	feet

Write

1. I have two —————.
2. The ————— has many leaves.
3. The ————— sits on the flower.
4. A hunter shoots —————.

Draw a bee and write a
sentence about it.

ea

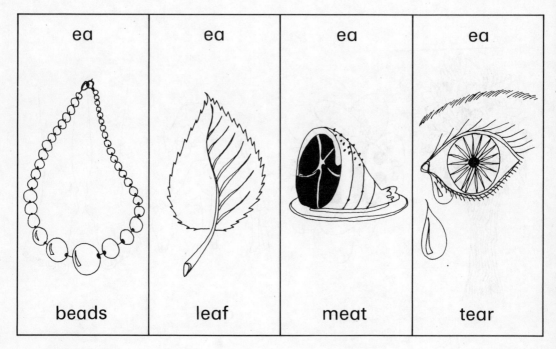

ea	ea	ea	ea
beads	leaf	meat	tear

Write

1. We have ——— for our dinner.
2. My Mum has lovely ———.
3. A ——— is green.
4. When I cry, a ——— runs
   down my cheek.

Write a sentence using

1. tea   2. heat

ee or ea

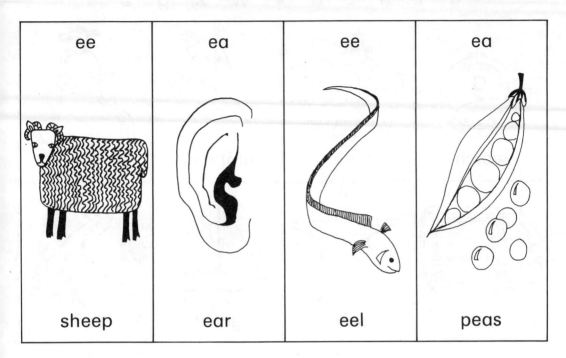

ee	ea	ee	ea
sheep	ear	eel	peas

Write

1. A woolly —— lives on a farm.

2. I use my —— to hear.

3. An —— is long and black.

4. My Mum put green ——
    on my plate.

Write a sentence using

1. sea   2. seeds

Find the word

q r s t u v w x y z

watch	queen	umbrella	tap
van	star	yacht	road

Write

q is for ——.   u is for ——.
r is for ——.   v is for ——.
s is for ——.   w is for ——.
t is for ——.   y is for ——.

a b —— —— e f —— —— —— j
k —— m n o —— q r —— ——
—— v w x —— ——.

ai

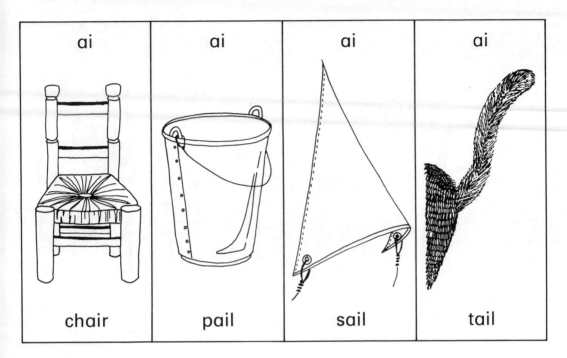

ai	ai	ai	ai
chair	pail	sail	tail

Write

1. Fill the ——— up with water.
2. The boat has a ———.
3. The cat has a big bushy ———.
4. I sit on a ——— in the room.

Draw a train on the rails.
Write a sentence about your train.

ay

ay	ay	ay	ay
tray	rays	hay	play

Write

1. The sun has lots of ———.
2. The farmer keeps ——— in the barn.
3. Put the cup on the ———.
4. I ——— on the swings.

Write a sentence using these words

1. pay   2. day

Where do these animals live?

kennel

nest

hive

bowl

sty

hole

Write

1. The bird lives in a ———.
2. A pink pig lives in a ———.
3. My pet fish lives in a ———.
4. The buzzing bee lives in a ———.
5. Some dogs live in a ———.
6. A little mouse ran into a ———.

Read these words

tree	hay	beads
hair	seat	pray

Draw a picture for each one.

Write

1. The farmer made a big —— stack.
2. There are no leaves on the ——.

Now you have to write a sentence for

3. beads
4. hair
5. pray
6. seat

oa

| oa | oa | oa | oa |
| coat | soap | boat | loaf |

Write

1. When I wash, I use a bar of ———.
2. We buy a fresh ——— from the shop.
3. The ——— sails on the blue sea.
4. My ——— has a hood and buttons.

Write a sentence using

1. road   2. toad

ow

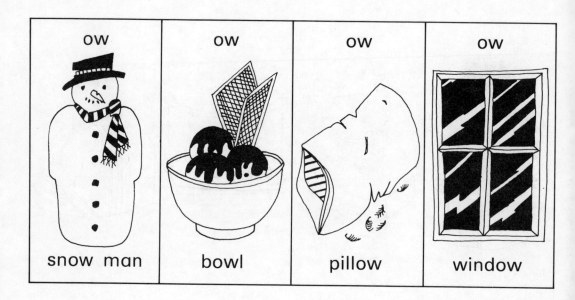

ow	ow	ow	ow
snow man	bowl	pillow	window

Write

1. In winter time, I made a ——
   in the garden.
2. The —— was full of ice cream.
3. When I look out of the ——, I
   can see the road.
4. I have a big, soft —— in my bed.

Write a sentence using these words

1. arrow   2. grow

Colours

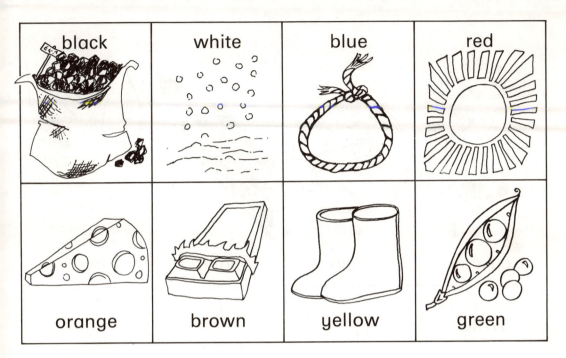

black	white	blue	red
orange	brown	yellow	green

Write

1. Snow is ——.

2. The loop is ——.

3. Coal is ——.

4. The sun is ——.

5. The boots are ——.

6. Peas are ——.

7. Cheese is ——.

8. A bar of chocolate is ——.

oi

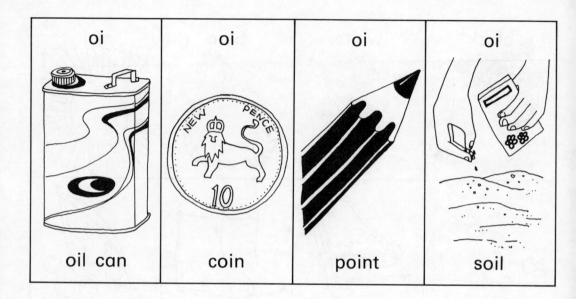

| oi | oi | oi | oi |
| oil can | coin | point | soil |

Write

1. My pencil has a very sharp ———.
2. We plant seeds in the dark ———.
3. The ——— ——— is full of oil.
4. The 10p ——— is round, silver and shiny.

Write a sentence using these words

1. joiner   2. boil

oy

Write

1. Santa left us lots of ———.
2. The ——— is playing football.

oi or oy

Read these words

join   Roy   boil   joy

Write about each word.

Read these words

bowl   arrow   toys

load   point   cloak

Draw a picture for each one.

Write

1. The men ———— the lorry with
    heavy things.
2. We must not ———— our finger at
    some one.

Now you have to write a sentence for

3. bowl
4. toys
5. arrow
6. cloak

Match

Look at the pictures. Read the words.

coat	mouse	fork
saucer	sugar	pepper

Draw and write

1. hat and coat.

2. cat and ———.

3. salt and ———.

4. knife and ———.

5. cup and ———.

6. milk and ———.

Read these sounds

ee	oi	ay	oo	sh	ch
wh	ai	ow	ea	oa	th

Draw the pictures and put in the
correct sounds to make the words.

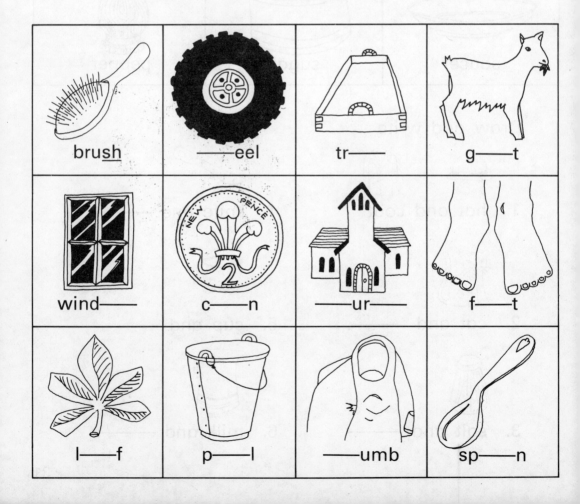

brush	—eel	tr——	g—t
wind——	c——n	——ur——	f——t
l——f	p——l	——umb	sp——n